Some Days Are Ashes

Poems, Limericks and Illustrations
By Christian DeWild

All poems, limericks and illustrations are Copyright Christian DeWild
2018

Thank you

Rita Cantergiani
My elementary school teacher whom
I consider family. Thank you for your tireless
efforts in getting this kid to read.

Mr. Anthony
For introducing me to the works
of Edgar Allen Poe in the 8th grade.

My family
Far and near, gone and here.
Too many people and reasons to list on this page.
I love you all

"The Not So Wicked Witch"
Inspired by Nancy Tovar

Edited by Stephanie Tebbs and Andy DeWild
Cover text by Melanie Hoppe

All people, names, incidents, stories and illustrations are all made up and based on fictional characters.

All poems, limericks and illustrations are copyright Christian DeWild 2018.

ISBN-13: 978-1-7337707-0-5
christiandewild@yahoo.com

Chapter I

Some Days Are Ashes

Martin's In The Mortuary
Unfit Vampire
I Fell In Love With A Zombie Girl
Daddy Loves Mummy
Me And You A Bit Askew
The Clumsy Ghost
Susan Strands Smells Her Hands
Vincent Rose
Alone In The Crowd
Bad Breath Phone
Eyeball On My Plate
Taxidermy Cat
Bleak Lenore
Some Days Are Ashes
A Broken Heart
Morbid Lester
I finally Got...
The Whistling, Tickling Nose Hair
The Sandman
The Unfortunate Witch
Broken
All The I Love You's I Never Said
Dreadful Mary

Ever So Sad Sally
Lobotomy
Monsters In My Head
The Ghastly Of All Ghastly Things
Stitched Up Black Bird
Dancing Skeletons
The Not So Wicked Witch
I Walked Into A Spider Web
Flip Flops
Hard Boiled Egg
Nose Hairs - O – Plenty
Every Piece Of Gum
Able To Fly
Melancholy Sue
Desmond DeCry
Jugular Glee
Loathsome Annie
I Can Be Loved Again
Monster Magnet
Gravestones
Three Legged Spider
Decrepit Pie
Lobotomy Lou
Peg Leg Pete
Sometimes I Laugh So Hard I Fart
Socks
I Found A Chair On The Freeway
The Stars
There Once Was A Fairy Princess

The Little Boy Who Couldn't Say Thank You
They're Trying To Break The Wishbone
There Once Was A Girl
Squandered Youth

Chapter II

Misery Ensues

Grotesque Amelia
Gloomy Garret
Creepy Norbert
Organizing Beetles
Vomiting Flies
Misery Ensues
Dark Pictures
I Don't Think Anymore
Monster In My House
Fumbling, Bumbling, Mumbling Man
Creepy Uncle
The Late Mr. Robbins
The Late Miss Macbeth
Grandfather Clock
Down The Drain
Misery Ensues Lou
Mournful Maggie
Decapitated Ted
I Gave You My Heart
I Brought My Love Some Flowers
Ode To A Sucker
Slippery Snot
The Boy Who Flung Boogers

The Flatulent Ghost
Wrapped Up Mummy
Witch In A Tree
The Discouraged Vampire
Monster In The Attic
Dog
Doll
Sorrowful Jane
Wicked Garden
Mortuary Poems
Rat-A-Tat-Tat
Ratsicle
Wrinkled Mummy
Jack-O-Lantern
Lady Medusa
Beautiful When You Sleep
Ever So Lonely Nate
The Widow In The Park
Victor The Vampire
The Cackling Cauldron
The Wrong Way Witch
Norman The Skull
The Escalator Poem
Mr. Toffin
Sometimes We Break

Chapter III

Dreadful Ways

Picnic
Descending Edgar
Spooky Things
Raggedy, Raggedy
Pendulum Ann
Doll Heads
Mr. Lear
There Once Was A Boy
One Week Band-Aid
Snakes In The Toilet
Plastic Spoons
The Couch Was A Monster
Dreadful Ways
Little Miss Forever Tears
Lonely Girl
But A Lonely Old Bed
Goodnight Poem
Lonely Tarantula
Menacing Earwig
Crunchy Roach
Goo Goblin Soup
Seven Goblins
Miserably, Drizzerbly, Dismally Do

Pieces Of Five
The Wickedly, Crookedly, Conniving Old Cat
Bird Cage Bat
Stitches The Dog
Spooky Carol
The Cryptic Potato
The Angry Pumpkin
Meatloaf
Lost Brain
My Miserable Companion
Misery Ensues Two
The Late Victoria Spears
Apologies
Valentine's Day
All Out Of Coffee
Otherwise I'd Be Alone
Montgomery Hall
Posthumous Chris
The Late Mr. Huffing
Mr. Mc Fry's Two Foggy Eyes
Out Of All The Ghosts
The Bearskin Rug

Chapter I

Martin's In The Mortuary

Martin's in the mortuary
Playing with the sheets
Pretending he's a ghost
While people try to sleep

Unfit Vampire

The vampire crawled through the window
And he stood over the bed
He thought for a moment
Then scratched his head
He leaned toward his victim
But he fainted instead
Cuz any sight of blood
Made him light in the head

I Fell In Love With A Zombie Girl

I fell in love with a zombie girl
And she liked me for my mind
We took long walks in the cemetery
After day time turned to night
She let me talk for hours
Telling stories of my life
She smiled and listened quietly
Paid no attention to the time

We walked together everywhere
Clear skies or in the rain
But only in the evening hours
Never in the day
I asked her if she'd marry me
But after long restrain
She said she didn't love me
She only loved my brain

Me And You A Bit Askew

I'm broken, she's broken
And he's broken too
We're all little bit askew
From the way we talk
To the things we do
Nobody's normal
Not me and not you

The Clumsy Ghost

Here he comes, there he goes
There he was, the clumsy ghost
Where he's been you'll always know
Things get broken where he goes
Knocking chairs, hitting walls
Crooked pictures down the hall
Getting bruises as a ghost
Is not an easy task you know
He's got fingers, he's got toes
And now he has a bloody nose
Locked himself outside last night
Couldn't find a way inside
Every door and window tried
Finally giving up he cried
"At times like these I hate my life!!"
Asked each and every passerby
Even though it hurt his pride
If they knew a way inside
Every time he was denied
People just don't like to pry
In anybody else's life

Even during times of strife
Here he comes, there he hides
Breaking everything in sight
But still clumsy ghost still tries
But now he strictly tries outside

Susan Strands Smells Her Hands

Susan Strands smells her hands
After everything she touches
She smells her fingers
After dinners, morning tea and lunches
Scents and smells and finger nails
Sniffs them by the bunches
Susan Strands smells her hands
And soaks scents up like sponges

In the bathroom, out again
Smells her newly unwashed hands
Blows her nose, smells the tissue
Drops it in the garbage can
Smells the boogers in her nose
Redundant, yes I understand
Susan Strands with her own brand
Of very sticky, smelly hands

Vincent Rose

Vincent Rose
Picks his nose
Every single
Place he goes
When he stops
No one knows
But that is just
Ol' Peter Rose
Digs his finger
Deep inside
So far up
His knuckle hides
He pushes in
And doesn't stop it
Reaches up to
His eye socket

Alone In The Crowd

I'm not very quiet
But I'm not very loud
Yet I still feel
Alone in the crowd

It's not like I have
My head in the clouds
Yet I still feel
Alone in the crowd

Got both of my feet
Firm on the ground
Yet I still feel
Alone in the crowd

I'm not quite complaining
Just thinking out loud
Why do I feel
Alone in the crowd?

Blank Page

Bad Breath Phone

Somebody left
Their very bad breath
On the speaking side of the phone

They left their stench
Their germ ridden drench
On the talking part of the phone

Their vile laden smell
Their sickly exhale
On the saying part of the phone

Their tooth decay
In a sensory way
On the voicing part of the phone

There's An Eyeball On My Plate

There's an eyeball on my plate
And it's staring right at me
It looks just like a grape
With abnormalities
I don't know how it got here
In fact I'm quite perplexed
One question that comes to mind is
What do I do next?
I've been told to mind my manners
My P's and My Q's
But there's an eyeball on my plate
What am I supposed to do?

TAXIDERMY CAT

Taxidermy cat doesn't play anymore
The poor old thing doesn't leave the floor
She used to play and she used to purr
But that was back when she still had fur
She spends her days just lying about
Ever since she fell off the couch
She used to take two meals a day
She hasn't eaten for nine years straight
My concern has gone to acceptance now
I no longer expect to hear her meow
Taxidermy cat doesn't play anymore more
I'm afraid she's become a bore

Bleak Lenore

Bleak Lenore
Lay on the floor
Staring at the ceiling
Like every day before
Looking at a crack
Imperfection or a score
Something else broken
Or anything more
Like everything else
In the world of Lenore

SOME DAYS ARE ASHES

Some days are ashes
Some days are dirt
I'm either in a coffin
Or stuck inside an urn

A Broken Heart

A broken heart
Is still a heart
It's the same size together
As it is apart

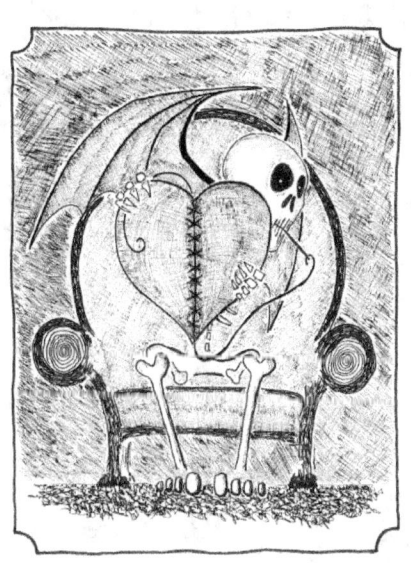

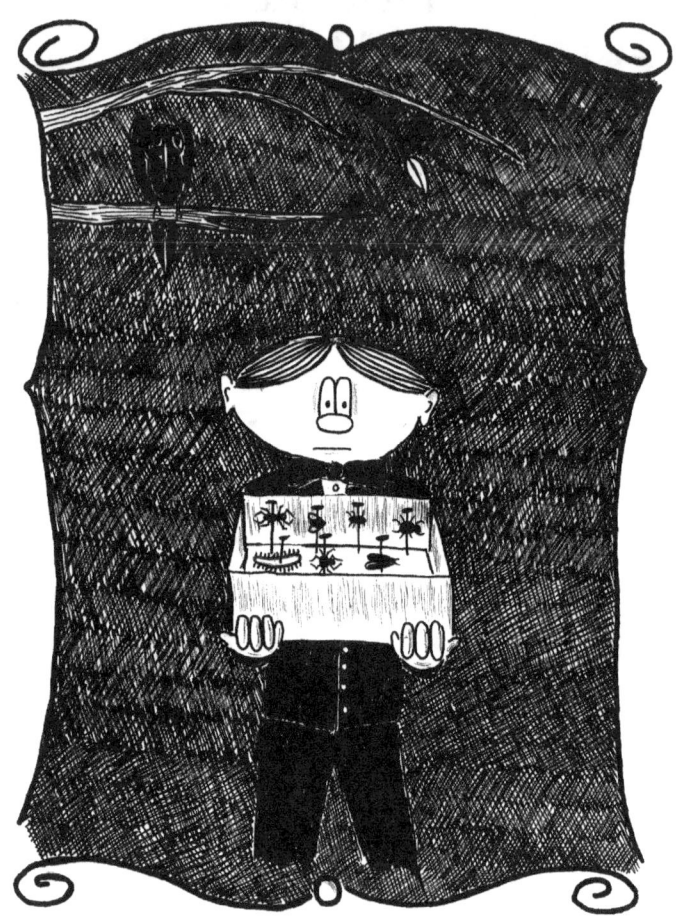

Morbid Lester

Morbid Lester
And his little dead bugs
Kept in a shoe box
Under the rug
Made up a name
For each little one
Pinned them with a needle
So they couldn't run

Morbid Lester
And his little dead bugs
Were delicate in stature
And brittle to the touch
But that didn't stop him
From showing them love
With a kiss on the head
Of each and every one

Morbid Lester
And his little dead bugs
Used to take walks
In the morning sun
They in their box
Held in his hands
He walking tall
Like a little proud man

Morbid Lester
And his little dead bugs
Were happy as can be
Till a crow from above
Swooped down upon them
And with a quick little tug
Snatched away the box
Of little dead bugs

Morbid Lester
Without his little dead bugs
Was sad and alone
With nothing left to love
So he sat in his room
And he noticed by his rug
That there on his back
Was a dying little bug

I Finally Got...

I've got a big Cadillac
Been saving all my life
Finally got to drive it home
The very day I died

I've got a big Cadillac
I really do deserve
The only problem that I find
Is this Cadillac's a hearse

The Whistling, Tickling Nose Hair

There's a hair in my nose
That tickles and whistles
With every breath that I take

It tickles and whistles
And sounds like a missile
With every breath in the day

Fired up like a pistol
I'm mad at this bristle
And all of its whistling ways

I'll find it and pull it
And knowing that this'll
Put an end to its whistling days

The Sandman

I woke up this morning
Jumped out of bed
Fell over forwards
Right down on my head
What new misfortune?
What happened last night?
I can't see a thing
Can't open my eyes
They're stuck to a close
Cemented it seems
There's crust on the edges
And inside the seams
There's grime in the crust
And goo in the grime
The sandman was here
During allergy time

The Unfortunate Witch

The unfortunate witch
From old Waterloo
Did not have a friend
Among the witches she knew
Did not have a witch
That she could talk to
Did not have a witch
Whom wouldn't be rude
They all thought her strange
Without any clue
They all called her "different"
And not of their crew
So she finally gave up
And they split off in two
Her on her rake
And them on their brooms

Broken

You're broken
I'm broken too
Let's put our pieces together
And start ourselves anew

All The I love You's I Never Said

Everybody I know will someday be dead
This I know in my heart and my head
This sometimes keeps me awake in bed
I think of all the I love you's I never said

Dreadful Mary

Dreadful Mary
Your smile is undone
Your eyes are black
And their paint has run
Down to your neck
By way of your cheeks
A puddle is forming
Right by your feet

Dreadful Mary
What has been done
To blow out your candle
Diminish your sun?
What do you do
When you are the one
Not to run to
But to run away from?

Ever-So-Sad Sally

Some people are mad and angry
Some people are moody and crabby
Some people are just plain happy
And then there's ever-so-sad Sally

Lobotomy

Lobotomy, Loboto-you
Someone stole my brain already
Don't you bother trying to

Monsters In My Head

Monsters in my closet
And underneath my bed
Monsters in the attic
And upstairs in my head
Monsters keep me up at night
Remembering things I've said
Reminding me of things I've done
And things that I regret

The Ghastly Of All Ghastly Things

The ghastly of all ghastly things
The frightening and most frightful scene
The hauntingly most haunting being
Is staring through the mirror at me

Stitched Up Blackbird

There once was a black bird
That used to be free
But he was shot down
And stuffed to the seams
He was stitched together
By a sewing machine
Then placed on the wall
For everybody to see

Dancing Skeletons

Dancing skeletons
All in a row
Dancing fingers
Dancing toes
Happy little bones
On a frail torso
Dancing skeletons
All in a row

Grab your partner
Do-si-do
Chatter those teeth
And raddle them bones
Dancing skeletons
All in a row

The sun goes down
The moon is a glow
Out of the dirt
And on to their toes
Dancing skeletons
All in a row

Cemetery waltz
With a partner in tow
The light of the moon
Makes shadows grow
Dancing skeletons
All in a row

Blank Page

The Not So Wicked Witch

The not so wicked witch
Of Arundel elementary
Wasn't really mean at all
In fact she was quite friendly

She had a wicked nose
A wart atop her chin
She even had one of those
Mean old wicked grins

She came into my class
Each and every Halloween
And passsed around to every child
A plastic spider ring

The not so wicked witch
Of Arundel elementary
Wasn't really mean at all
In fact she was quite funny

I Walked Into A Spider Web

I walked into a spider web
Frantically I wiped my head
I flailed my arms and kicked the air
Screamed until my lungs were bare
I cried, I ran with incredible speed
Tripped on my foot, fell on some weeds
Caught by surprise I started to pee
All over my pants, my knees and my feet
I pulled my hair and hoped to find
Every trace of spider twine
And after that I think I'll try
To find a pair of pants that's dry.

Flip Flops

You don't realize
How loud flip flops can be
Until you are walking
In a Quiet library

Hardboiled Egg

Hardboiled egg, it's just me and you
Is your shell going to break into a million tiny pieces?
Or can we just make it two?

Nose Hairs - O - Plenty

I've got nose hairs - O - plenty
Nose hairs galore
I've got nose hairs that gracefully
Drape to the floor

They used to be brown
But now that I've aged
They seem to be more
Of a deep brownish grey

My nose hairs are tangled
They seem quite a mess
For birds in the spring
They make a fine nest

My nose hairs get caught
In my food when I dine
Have you ever chomped into
A hair Sheppard's pie?

They do come in handy
When being discrete
I pull out a long one
And start flossing my teeth

Blank Page

Every Piece Of Gum

When I was just a little boy
I used to swallow my gum
I'd only chew it for a bit
And then I would be done
I'd swallow the pieces down
Right to my very gut
But what I failed to realize
It was there that it got stuck
And every other piece of gum
I swallowed when I thought was done
Had all collected one by one
And has become so cumbersome
I could have spit them on someone
But no, I swallowed all my gum
And now I'm sick and that's no fun
They'll probably have to check my bum
In front of each and every one
To find this mass collected gum
They'll have to get each piece undone
Then collect the entire sum
Just because my mother's son
Had swallowed every piece of gum

Able To Fly

There once was a boy
Who wished he could fly
But he didn't have wings
Or an appendage to try
He wished really hard
And still was denied
So he thought of a plan
To help him take flight
He'd capture and go
Rip wings off of flies
Eat them for supper
And then in good time
Maybe he too
Would be able to fly

Melancholy Sue

Melancholy Sue
And her melancholy view
Everything so tragic
Every mood is blue

Melancholy Sue
And her melancholy blues
Never had a friend
To share her melancholy news

Melancholy Sue
And her melancholy news
Of everything so tragic
From her melancholy view

Melancholy Sue
And her melancholy view
Always kept on walking
In her melancholy shoes

Melancholy Sue
In her melancholy shoes
Always kept on tripping
Over Melancholy Sue

Desmond DeCry

Desmond DeCry
With never a smile
Sat in his chair
And waited awhile
He waited for someone,
Some way or something
To deeply offend him
Beyond his belief
Something so big
Or something so small
It didn't matter
He'd still be appalled

Jugular Glee

Jugular Glee
The broken clown
With the sad old eyes
And a smiling frown
How do you smile
When it's upside down
And laugh like a cry
Then the other way around?

Loathsome Anny

Loathsome Anny
Was tired of the day
So she took a brush
And painted it away
She used some purples
She used some greys
In very wide strokes
She covered the page
From top to bottom
And all points between
There couldn't be found
A blue or a green
No blue for the sky
No green for the grass
Just purple and grey
No other contrasts

I Can Be Loved Again

I've got a cobwebbed heart
And a dusty brain
And the tips of my fingers
Are weathered and stained
But I do believe
I can be loved again
Yes, I do believe
I can be loved again

I've got a crooked soul
Always waiting for the rain
And the smile on my face
Will surely fade away
But I do believe
I can be loved again
Yes, I do believe
I can be loved again

Ya, I'm just like you
And you're just like me
We go hand and hand
Like vultures in the trees
But I do believe
I can be loved again
Yes, I do believe
I can be loved again

Monster Magnet

I have a fear
I have a habit
I think I am
A monster magnet

Not on purpose
Not for show
They seem to be
Everywhere I go

Some are large
Some are small
Some I can't
Even see at all

Green ones, black ones
Yellow and red
Some with jelly
Oozing from their heads

Grave Stones

Grave stones
Broken bones
Mallet finger
Xylophone
Ghost moan
Zombie groan
Let them cast
The first stone
Don't slow
Run home
You don't wanna
Be alone
Some way
Somewhere
We all have a
Gravestone

Three Legged Spider

Nothing would be more terrifying
Nothing could be less finer
Than to have the misfortune
Of being a three legged spider

It would be devastating
I'd probably be annoyed
If I actually were
A three legged arachnoid

Lobotomy Lou

Lobotomy Lou
Had no clue
How to count
From one to two
What misery
He couldn't see
How to go
From two to three
Furthermore
The dreadful bore
Couldn't jump
From three to four
As no surprise
The poor old guy
Couldn't climb
From four to five
In clueless bliss
He smiles and sits
With no attempt
To count to six
If he were Evan
Or perhaps Kevin
He'd be able to count
From one to seven
But I'm sorry to say
That in Lou's state
He can't even count
From seven to eight

It should be a crime
And it wouldn't be mine
That Lou doesn't know
About number nine
So we wasted the day
And our time's at an end
But Lou wouldn't know
That his curfew is ten

Peg Leg Pete

Peg Leg Pete
Was a pirate of the sea
With a gravely odd
Number of feet
Five full toes
And a stick from a tree
Make up the legend
Known as Peg Leg Pete

Sometimes I Laugh So Hard I Fart

Sometimes I laugh so hard I fart
Then laugh because I farted
And then I laugh again and fart
And end up where I started

Socks

Socks under cushions
Socks on the floor
Socks in the corner
Behind the bathroom door
I don't want to see
Your socks anymore
Put them away
In the wash or the drawer
If I see them again
You'll be crying to the store
Cuz you won't have
Your socks anymore
And I won't buy them
You'll have to do a chore
All because of
Socks on the floor

I Found A Chair On The Freeway

I found a chair on the freeway
But I'm struggling to find the matching set
There's someone out there somewhere
Who is struggling to seat a guest

The Stars

The stars are beautiful tonight
Hanging low from the evening sky
Oh, those are actually satellites
Forget it then, never mind

There Once Was A Fairy Princess

There once was a fairy princess
In a far, far away land
She waited for her prince
But he never showed up…the end

The Little Boy Who Couldn't Say Thank You

The little boy who couldn't say "thank you"
Couldn't say "please" or "hi, how do you do?"
Never said "you're welcome" but never had to
Because he never gave anyone anything of value

They're Trying To Break The Wishbone

They're trying to break the wishbone
They're prying it apart
They're trying to break the wishbone
It's breaking my heart
They're trying to break the wishbone
But what they don't see
Is the wishbone they're breaking
Is still inside me

There Once Was A Girl

There once was a girl
With a smile on her face
But as time did go by
That smile got erased
Then turned upside down
And now was replaced
By a bow in the lips
Or a frown as they say
It couldn't be fixed
Still there to this day
And I do miss the girl
With the smile on her face

Youth

My youth was squandered
By the child that I was

Blank Page

Chapter II

Grotesque Amelia

Grotesque Amelia
Flossed her teeth
Fed herself
Upon the meat
Left there hanging
On the string
Little pieces
Dangling
Grotesque Amelia
Flossed her teeth
For another
Meal to eat

Gloomy Garret

Gloomy Garret
Always had a frown
And everywhere he went
He was greeted by a cloud

Creepy Norbert

Creepy Norbert
This way comes
With his dead cat
Mitsy Crumbs
He's got fingers
He got thumbs
Holds the leash
She's dragging from
Didn't know that
She could fly
Till a gust of wind
Came by
Now Creepy Norbert
Has a kite
Boy is he
A lucky guy

Organizing Beetles

Organizing beetles
Arranging them by size
The big ones are the main course
The small ones are the sides

Vomiting Flies

Flies have to vomit
All over their food
To turn it into
Some kind of goo
That they can then eat
Because they can't chew
So keep this in mind
When they land on your food

Misery Ensues

Misery ensues
But I don't know what to do
Is misery into me?
Or is it misery that I'm into?

Dark Pictures

Painting dark pictures
It's just what I do
I'm done painting landscapes
Now I only paint ruins

I don't Think Anymore

I don't think anymore
It drove me to crazy
I don't think anymore
It drove me to stress
I don't think anymore
It made me too angry
The only thing is
I don't think any less

Monster In My House

There's a monster in my house, a monster indeed
But he is not scary, not vicious or mean
He is not angry, he's not even obscene
And I will admit that he's never been seen
But I know he exists, and it's not just a dream
Because whenever I leave I can't find my keys
They're never in the place I left them to be
So there must be a monster, a monster indeed

Fumbling, Bumbling, Mumbling Man

Fumbling, bumbling, mumbling man
Making mistakes as fast as he can
Trying to get everything done at once
Will only make a grumbling dunce

Creepy Uncle

Creepy uncle
Stares too long
Sticks his nose
Where it don't belong

Creepy uncle
Farts a lot
Blames it on me
When he's caught

Creepy uncle
Blows his nose
In a rag
He neatly folds

Creepy uncle
Is a mess
His clothes don't match
When he's actually dressed

The Late Miss Macbeth

Here lies
Joyce Macbeth
She talked so much
She ran out of breath

The Late Mr. Robbins

Here lies
The late Mr. Robbins
He ate so much
He took up two coffins

Grandfather Clock

There's no more room in the family plot
So grandpa's in the grandfather clock
We stop to see him twice a day
Check out the time and go on our way

Down The Drain

Mr. McKinley's daughter
Had a fear that was quite a bother
She thought she would go down the drain and drown
With the outgoing bathtub water

Misery Ensues Lou

Misery ensues Lou
Loved to plot his doom
He wasn't happy unless he was sad
And under a crippling gloom

Mournful Maggie

Mournful Maggie
Was so full of dread
That no other thoughts
Could fit in her head

Decapitated Ted

Decapitated Ted
Didn't have a head
His heart and brain would always fight
So it finally fled

His heart was not impressed
It jumped out of his chest
He doesn't have a head or heart
Now he's just a mess

I Gave You My Heart

I gave you my heart
Because I love you
I even mopped up the mess
So you wouldn't have to

I Brought My Love Some Flowers

I brought my love some flowers
She was happy as can be
Until she bent to smell them
And was stung by several bees

Ode To A Sucker

I dropped my sucker
Behind a chair
It picked up a cobweb
And it picked up some hair

It picked up a bug
Yes a fly that was it
But it all came right off
With a wipe and some spit

Slippery Snot

Slippery snot
I did not see you there
Alone on the table
Because of the glare

You were cold when we touched
Must have been there awhile
And now I can't lose you
You're cramping my style

Slippery snot why do you smear
And not go away?
You only damped the cloth
But on my arm you remain

I may let you dry
Then flick you away
But that kind of time
Would take most of the day

I think I'll just wipe you
On some passerby
And with this final thought
I bid you good-bye

The Boy Who Flung Boogers

Edmond was a boy
And very unique indeed
He liked to fling his boogers
On everyone he'd see
Sometimes he'd fling them far
Other times very close
Sometimes he'd aim for their hair
And sometimes just their clothes
One time he aimed really high
It peaked then dropped down south
And while his father lie down yawning
The booger hit his mouth

The Flatulent Ghost

The flatulent ghost
Of Misery Falls
Couldn't sneak up
On people at all
If you didn't smell him
Before he arrived
You certainly heard
His flatulent cry
Then instantly knew
You were not alone
And sadly again
His cover is blown

Wrapped Up Mummy

Wrapped up mummy
Passed a bathroom door
Someone needed toilet paper
Now he is no more

Witch In A Tree

What do I hear?
What do I see?
Looks like a witch
Stuck in my tree
How did she get there?
How can this be?
Must have been speeding
Must have indeed
And surely not looking
Or she would have seen
That towering structure
Known as a tree
Where it's always been
And always will be
She must have been speeding
Speeding indeed
Or else she wouldn't be
Stuck in that tree

The Discouraged Vampire

The discouraged vampire
With the squeaky coffin
Could not sneak away
Every so often
Without waking up
The mice and the bats
That live in the castle
Along with the rats
Who then would wake
The family upstairs
That lived in the castle
They unknowingly shared
Which led to the father
Stomping downstairs
Yelling at everyone
"Quiet down there!!"
Flipping the switches
Turning on lights
Making dad noises
And causing a fright

All the rats scatter
The bats and the mice
And the starving vampire
Stuck again for the night

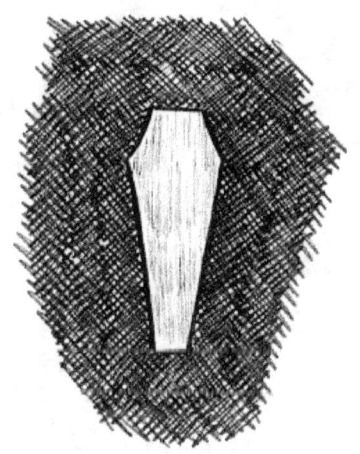

Monster In The Attic

There's a monster in the attic
That only moves at night
Making only little sounds
As not to cause a fright

Drinking little sips of water
That leak in from the roof
And feeding off of little spiders
He can chew on with his tooth

There's a monster in the attic
And he doesn't sleep at all
He stands in just one corner
Staring at the wall

Dog

My dog Lamar
Was hit by a car
Needless to say he was dead

The following day
His buried remains
Were dug up beside the shed

He was in the yard
Barking at cars
The drivers were stricken with dread

Oddly by far
My old dog Lamar
Had risen up from the dead

Doll

What would you do
If you woke up one night
And walked to the kitchen
To grab a quick bite
And there in your way
Was a doll on the rug
With her arms stretching out
Like she wanted a hug
???

Sorrowful Jane

This is the tale
Of sorrowful Jane
Who lived with her parents
Till they moved away

They found a new house
But Jane couldn't go
Cus she was a ghost
Who could never leave home

Wicked Garden

Sarah in the garden
Watering the plants
Dragged into a hole
And devoured by ants

Michael in the garden
Tangled in ivy
When they finally found him
He wasn't so lively

Adam in the garden
Thought he was so quick
Tripped himself running
Got impaled by a stick

Mortuary Poems

Norman went to the mortuary
To read his poems aloud
He knew that it was quiet
And he'd have a captive crowd

Blank Page

Rat-A-Tat-Tat

Rat-A-Tat-Tat
Thought he was a rat
But he has a pair of wings
Turns out he's a bat

Ratsicle

A frozen rat
Is just like a treat
The tail is the stem
You hold while you eat

Wrinkled Mummy

Wrinkled mummy
Broke out of his tomb
And wandered the city
All afternoon
He found an iron
A plug and a cord
All he needs now
Is an ironing board

Jack-O-Lantern

I'm a Jack-O-Lantern
Without a body
I'm just a head
In somebody's lobby
With a candle where
My brain used to be
One month a year
Just for free candy

Lady Medusa

Lady Medusa
Was always alone
All the men she loved
Got turned into stone

You're Beautiful When You Sleep

You're beautiful when you sleep
I love to watch you dream
But then you wake right up
And ruin everything

Ever So Lonely Nate

Ever so lonely Nate
Could never find a date
So he took a mannequin to be
His lawfully wedded mate

She couldn't bare him kids
But this he didn't miss
However he could do without
Splinters every time they kissed

The Widow In The Park

The widow in the park
Sitting all alone
Feeding all the pigeons
Before returning home

The widow in the park
Draped in black and grey
Walks down to her bench
Each and every day

The widow in the park
Spends the afternoon
Feeding all the pigeons
Pieces of her groom

Victor The Vampire

Victor the vampire
Was not like the rest
He was rather quite clumsy
I have to confess
He's simply small minded
And always distressed
His cape is quite wrinkled
His hair is a mess
His first attempt haunting
Was a dreadful affair
It took place at a house
Called the Chateau Le Mere
He slipped on a shirt
While haunting a boy
Then fell over backwards
And tripped on a toy
Now, this sent him flying
Into a closet door closed
Which lead him to nursing
A mess of a nose

His second attempt
Was not a success
He ran from a ghost
That was just a hung dress
This set him running
Scared down the hall
Where he fumbled across
An old creepy doll
That happened to be
Left on the floor
That was enough
He wanted no more
He left the chateau
In a terrible state
He tripped on his shoes
And over his cape
He's never returned
To haunting again
He's never been heard from
Ever since then

The Cackling Cauldron

The Cackling Cauldron
And it's bubbling goo
Loved making spells
That caused others gloom

The more evil the spell
The giddier it got
Oh my, oh my
What a no good old pot

What a dreadful steamer
What a horrible vat
A despicable boiler
To get joy out of that

To laugh at misfortune
To cause such undo
The Cackling Cauldron
And it's unfortunate brew

The Wrong Way Witch

The wrong way witch
In her way of never knowing
Wasn't ever sure
If she was coming or going

The wrong way witch
With her lines quite crossed
Always found the way
To getting herself lost

The wrong way witch
Out of shear distaste
Never seemed to fail
At getting quite misplaced

The wrong way witch
Who has always been mislead
Would've had much better luck
If she only stayed in bed

Norman The Skull

Norman the skull
Whose life was dull
Until he found out
He could roll down the hall

He didn't need a body
No feet and no toes
To get him to places
He wanted to go

To scare all the people
The patrons, the guests
By rolling around
And causing unrest

Many a screech
And many a yell
Would ever since come
From the Norman Hotel

The Escalator Poem

Poor old Emily Rose
The escalator took her toes
She didn't leap over the crack
Now she'll never get them back

Mr. Toffin

Here lies our
Dear Mr. Toffin
Done in by a splinter
He got making a coffin

Chapter III

Sometimes We Break

Sometimes we break
Sometimes we crumble
Sometimes we fall
Or we just stumble
But it's not how we break
And it's not how we fall
But how we get up
And how we stand tall
That means everything
At the end of it all

Picnic

While most people packed
A picnic for noon in the park
Mr. Wills packed one
For the cemetery after dark

Descending Edgar

Edgar was quiet
And painfully shy
He was always alone
Not a soul by his side

But Edgar drew weary
Of being alone
Whether in public
Or in his own home

So he went for a walk
To find a new mate
He passed by a graveyard
And stood at the gate

He decided to enter
And walk through the grounds
Till he came to a plot
Cleared the ground and sat down

The name on the stone
Was Lilly DuFrane
He said to the stone
"That's a beautiful name."

A voice from the dirt
Said "Thank you my dear."
"Why don't you come closer?
And sit over here?"

So Edger moved closer
But just by a foot
He'd much rather not
He'd prefer to stay put

"I beg you come closer
I can't hear you at all"
Said the voice once again
From the dirt she did call

So Edgar sat closer
And he said with a grin
"If I sit any closer
I might just fall in."

Suddenly a hand
Pushed out of the dirt
Clinching poor Edgar
By the sleeve of his shirt

Clinching poor Edgar
And dragging him down
Down passed the grass
And deep underground

And still to this day
He's under the stone
Marked Lilly DuFrane
Just them two alone

Blank Page

Spooky Things

Where do the spooky things go at night?
Why they go to the places where there is no light.
What do the spooky things do at night?
Why they spook and haunt and cause a fright
Where do the spooky things go in the day?
Why they hide in the cracks and the attics and caves
What do the spooky things do in the day?
Why they close their eyes and the sleep the day away

Raggedy, Raggedy

The raggedy witch
In the raggedy house
With her raggedy hat
And her raggedy blouse
Made a raggedy stew
In a raggedy pot
From the raggedy bones
Of the children she caught

Pendulum Ann

Pendulum Ann
Was caught in a jam
With her impending doom
Closely at hand

Little by little
And inch by inch
Pendulum Ann
Was sure in a pinch

Yes, I'm afraid
That she'll meet the blade
With no one around
To come to her aid

Pendulum Ann
Is finally at rest
But in two different places
My what a mess

Doll Heads

Mr. Ralls took heads off of dolls
And put them in frames all down the hall
He made up a story for each little head
He said they were family but long since quite dead

Mr. Lear

Mr. Lear
Picks his ear
And makes his
Earwax disappear

In a fashion
Quite unique
May be shocking
To the weak

Scraping earwax
With his teeth
From his finger
Carefully

Chewing, chomping
Never stopping
This behavior
Is quite shocking

Mr. Lear
Can finally hear
And his hunger
Has disappeared

There Once Was A Boy

There once a boy
Who would lick windows
When they layered with condensation

He said it was his way
Of tasting the outside
And curing dehydration

One Week Band Aid

I've been wearing this band aid for a week
I'll admit that is quite a streak
It's starting to fade, but the wound still remains
And I'm afraid it's starting to stink

Snakes In The Toilet

I read about snakes in the toilet
I read that they hide in the pipes
Be sure not to sit down long
Because I read that they like to bite

Plastic Spoons, Knives And Forks

Plastic spoons
And plastic forks
Plastic knives
Against the sporks

Spoons are for scooping
Knives, just to cut
Forks are for stabbing
And picking things up

But sporks do it all
So they win the wars
And this makes for jealous
Utensils in drawers

The Couch Was A Monster

The couch was a monster
Of which I distained
It swallowed more things
Than the old shower drain
It swallowed up pillows
Blankets and food
Under the cushions
Hidden from view
It swallowed up sox
And even a coat
I still haven't found
The tv remote

Dreadful Ways

No more sunshine
Only rain
From the view
Of my window pane

Window got sad
Pulled all the drapes
So she couldn't see the world
In its dreadful shape

Little Miss Forever Tears

Little miss
Forever tears
With a permanent frown
From ear to ear
Basking in
Her miserable fears
Without the means
In which to steer
Out of her mess
And out of her gloom
As a matter of fact
Even out of her room

Lonely Girl

Lonely girl
Did lonely things
All by herself
No company
All by herself
No friends to keep
All by herself
Less suffering
No companion
Boy or girl
Just the one
She deemed as loyal
Her, herself
And she alone
Never waiting
For the phone
Things are better
Just this way
Keeping everyone
Else at bay
Her alone
And that's the way
And in some ways
I can relate
It's easier
To be alone

Kids you'll see this
When you're grown
Sometimes you're stronger
On your own

But A Lonely Old Bed

The dead Mr. Gill
In life had his fill
Of money and things
My what a thrill
He swindled the rich
And stole from the poor
But is wasn't enough
He still wanted more
But the quest got him sick
And the sick got him dead
And now he has nothing
But a lonely old bed

Goodnight Poem

Goodnight full moon
In your sky way up high
Goodnight mom and dad
Tucked in your bed nice and tight
Goodnight stars
Flickering down oh so bright
And goodnight boogieman
Under the bed out of sight

The Lonely Tarantula

The lonely tarantula
Wanted a hug
So he crawled into bed
Where he could be snug
The person in bed
Wasn't so pleased
You could tell by the screams
And the puddle of pee

Menacing Earwig

Nighttime had fallen
And all were asleep
When the menacing earwig
Decided to creep
Creepily crawling
Into small beds
Inching his way
In ears and in heads
Enjoy your sweet dreams
While the evening wanes
Don't think of the earwigs
Eating your brains

Crunchy Roach

Crunchy roach
Is good on toast
Or maybe an egg
That's boiled or poached

Crunchy roach
Is good alone
With a cup of tea
And a toasted scone

Goo, Goblin Soup

Goo, goblin soup
Is more of a stew
With all of its goop
And all of its goo
Not quite a soup
Like I ever knew
But more like a stew
Or maybe a roux
With things to be chewed
Not slurped like a brew
But how would I know
And who ever knew
That I'd be the goblin
In Goo, Goblin stew.

Seven Goblins

Seven goblins
One, two, three
Plus four more
For company
Seven goblins
Join a heist
Tired of eating
Little mice
Seven goblins
Sick of bait
Want small children
On their plate
Seven goblins
In the woods
Found a cottage
Full of goods
Son and daughter
Mom and dad
Seven goblins
And two bags
Two bags full

And out the door
Mom and dad
Sleep and snore
Seven goblins
With a match

Make a fire
And cook a batch
With a cauldron
And a spoon
Dinner coming
Very soon
Seven goblins
Five plus four
Don't feel hungry
Any more

Miserably, Drizzerbly, Dismally Do

Miserably, drizzerbly, dismally doo
Can I be miserably, dismally too?
Just miserably me and dismally you
Or dismally one and miserably two
Miserably content in this dismally zoo
Two peas in a pod from this dismally shrew
Limping along in our dismally shoes
Miserably, drizzerbly, dismally doo

In Pieces of Five

Mrs. Platt
Sewed her cat
After it strayed
To the railroad track

Train came along
Took all nine lives
Had to pick it up
In pieces of five

With twine and a pin
Dived right in
Now the cat's been named
As her next of kin

Mrs. Platt
Caught a draft
Died in bed
The day after that

Cat got it all
The roof and the walls
And poor Mr. Platt
Got the old withdrawals

The Wickedly, Crookedly, Conniving Old Cat

The wickedly, crookedly, conniving old cat
Contemplating crookedness and other such acts
Contemplating crookedness and that is a fact
What a wickedly, crookedly, conniving old rat

Birdcage Bat

Mrs. Black
Keeps a bat
In a birdcage
At her flat

Thought it was
A little bird
Yes, I know
It sounds absurd

But she is old
She doesn't know
So we never
Told her so

Stiches The Dog

Stiches the dog
Wondered his way
Passed an old seamstress
One winter's day
The seamstress was spinning
Her needle and thread
Until it ran out
The roll came to an end
She found an old strand
There on the ground
And was off again spinning
While Stiches unwound

Spooky Carol

Spooky Carol
Loved her pets
But she hugged them
All to death

She loved too much
And love can hurt
Just go ask
Her hamster Bert

The Cryptic Potato

The cryptic potato
In the cupboard it stayed
Hour after hour
And day after day
Until several months
Passed for the spud
It started to sprout
Three or four buds
These buds grew much bigger
Than the cupboards confines
And out reached the spud
To cause the demise
Of the little old lady
That lived there alone
And brought the potato
To rot in her home

The Angry Pumpkin

Angry pumpkin
Why do you frown?
Why do you scowl
And furl your brow?

Angry pumpkin
To me he did say
It's not my fault
Someone carved me this way

Meatloaf

Mother made meatloaf
Like nobody else
She didn't use meat
That was frozen or shelved
But I did one day notice
Something not right
We kept losing neighbors
Night after night
At first it was dogs
And then it was cats
Not before long
It was Mr. Labatts
Mrs. Labatts
Did not have a clue
That her husband
Was cooked at 452

Lost Brain

Mr. McLane
Lost his brain
Little by little
As it did drain
Out of his nose
Just like rain
Down the glass
Windowpane
Against his shirt
And left a stain
Every noodle
Like a chain
Spilling down
Again and again
Till there was nothing
Left to drain
Mr. McLane
Lost his brain

My Miserable Companion

My miserable companion
Stood on the lawn
Staring at puddles
All winter long

My miserable companion
Picked off a scab
Put it in water
Cus it looked like a crab

My miserable companion
Snorted a fly
To feel the wings tickle
Him from inside

My miserable companion
Squeezes his nose
To harvest the white stuff
Before the pores close

My miserable companion
On night in the fall
Licked every light switch
In the grand hall

My miserable companion
Never discrete
When biting his warts
Off of his feet

Misery Ensues Two

Misery ensues two
And I don't know what to do
When misery comes
And I come undone
How do I rise from the gloom?

The Late Victoria Spears

Here Lies
Victoria Spears
She cried so much
She drowned in her tears

Apologies

She apologized when she was wrong
She apologized when she was right
She apologized just to apologize
Just to end a fight

Valentine's Day

We broke up on Valentine's Day
The love we had just couldn't be saved
By a box of chocolates
And a flower bouquet

All Out Of Coffee

Sink full of dishes
And my head's still foggy
Can't find the sponge
And we're all out of coffee

Otherwise I'd Be All Alone

There's a blanket of leaves above me
A pillow of dirt below
Roots from a tree to hold me
Otherwise I'd be all alone

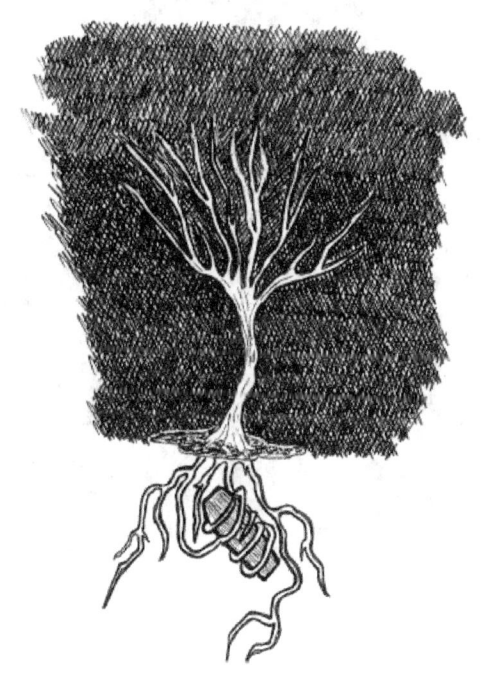

Montgomery Hall

Montgomery Hall
Was extremely tall
He wouldn't fit into
A coffin at all

Special arrangements
Were put into play
To make one his size
Where he could comfortably lay

The casket was longer
Than originally thought
Much longer indeed
Than would fit in the plot

They dropped it in vertically
Then buried the box
And if you walk by
You can still see the top

Posthumous Chris

Posthumous Chris
Caused quite a tiff
He attended his service
Disguised as a stiff

The guests were appalled
And quite at a loss
When they all were found mourning
An empty old box

They banned him for life
Which is odd in a way
And he was never allowed
To see his own grave

The Late Mr. Huffing

Here should lay
Mr. Huffing
He caught poison oak
And scratched himself to nothing

Mr. Mc Fry's Two Foggy Eyes

Mr. Mc Fry's
Two foggy eyes
Became quite a burden
Since he broke down and cried

Over the woman
Who broke his poor heart
It was all over quick
Before it could start

He got out a cleaner
For windows and glass
And wiped clean his eyes
With a soft moistened rag

He thought it would help
His crying for sure
His heart's really be broken
Cause he's crying some more

Out Of All The Ghosts

I'm trying to sleep
But there's a ghost in the hall
Dragging his chains
From wall to wall

I take my pillow
I cover my head
But I still hear the sound
Of chains from my bed

I shove my fingers
Into my ears
But this does nothing
The sound is still here

So I lay in bed
In disbelief
Nothing to do
And no way to sleep

Out of all the ghosts
From the cities to the plains
Why do I get
The ghost who has chains?

The Bearskin Rug

The bearskin rug
That lay on the floor
In the parlor
Beside the door
Just ate our dog
To our surprise
Right before
Our very eyes
Grandpa swore
That it was dead
Should have just
Kept the head
And hung it up
Upon the wall
Wouldn't be in
This mess at all
Now the bear
Is after Paul
Chased him out
Into the hall

Has to be
The only rug
To ever have eaten
The family pug
And the last
Child born

To this family
Ever scorned
All because
Our Grandpa Doug
Had to have
A bearskin rug

The End

www.ingramcontent.com/pod-product-compliance
Lightning Source LLC
Chambersburg PA
CBHW071156070526
44584CB00019B/2814